CW00684225

Against Equality

Don't Ask to Fight Their Wars

Against Equality is art and publishing collective dispersed across the United States and Canada. Together we manage an online archive of critical texts and visual culture devoted to queer and trans critiques of the neoliberal mainstream gay and lesbian politics of inclusion. These texts focus on gay marriage, gays in the military and hate crimes legislation.

This archive can be accessed online at

www.againstequality.org

Against Equality

Don't Ask to Fight Their Wars

Edited by Ryan Conrad

Published by:

Against Equality Publishing Collective, 8 Howe Street, Lewiston ME 04240.

Cover design by:

Chris Vargas - www.chrisevargas.com

Dedicated to all the queer and trans folks
engaged in the desperate search for our
most fantastic queer histories…

CONTENTS

Acknowledgments

Acknowledgements

This project would not have been possible without the endless hours of writing and editing done by all our contributors and those that continue to take a chance on publishing our work. Many thanks to Common Dreams, Counter Punch, No More Potlucks, The Guide, Pink Triangle Press, Windy City Times, AK Press, and the numerous personal blogs on which our work has been posted and re-posted. Additional gratitude goes to Yasmin Nair and Deena Loeffler for their many hours of proofreading and exquisite humor.

"Community Spirit": The New Gay Patriot and the Right to Fight in Unjust Wars

Mattilda Bernstein Sycamore

An Introduction

I remember when the U.S. started bombing Iraq under the first President Bush. I was a senior in high school, studying for exams at the American University student center. For some reason, that's where disaffected outlaw kids at Washington, DC private schools went to study, maybe because you could smoke inside, and you could buy alcohol without ID, and I guess our schools were right nearby, but I had to drive a half hour to get there: I was trying really hard to fit in at not fitting in. I looked up at one of the TV screens flashing news updates, and the bombs were going off. That's how I remember it, anyway. My whole body went hot and then cold — I couldn't possibly study anymore; there was no point.

I went to the big antiwar demos in DC, enthralled by the possibilities of public protest, studying the pageantry and anger of the banners and costumes, designing my own handmade signs, taking pictures of my sister and a friend holding up their fingers to make peace in front of cops in riot gear. I watched the protests in other cities on the news, keeping track of the places with the most people out in the street. This was one of the first times that San Francisco entered my world view — there were as many people protesting there as in New York, even though I knew San Francisco was a tenth of the size.

Soon yellow ribbons appeared inside the avowedly liberal school in affluent Northwest DC that I had attended since second grade — I couldn't believe the hypocrisy. How could you support the troops if you opposed the war? To me, every soldier was a cold-blooded killer. Later, once I realized it was poor and working class people, many of them people of color, sent around the world as cannon fodder, I would modify this stance to welcome deserters, those who came back from fighting to piece together their lives as antiwar activists, and anyone trying desperately to get out of the U.S. killing machine. Nevertheless, the pro-military antiwar agenda eagerly trumpeted in every left media outlet still leaves quite a bit to be desired: how will we ever end vicious wars of aggression if most of the experts we hear from aren't antiwar at all, but only speaking about why this particular war is unjust or badly organized?

I ended up in San Francisco sooner than I expected, after a year at the elite university I'd spent my whole life working towards, a place where everything I learned I discovered outside of class. I learned how to call myself queer, how to build a protest movement for racial and economic justice at a so-called liberal institution that still officially denied entrance to students based on their inability to pay. I helped to organize a building takeover that led to hundreds of arrests, months of protests, and national news. This was the culmination of years of student activism, but still it led to no tangible change because the administration didn't really care, and that's where I learned the most.

I left college to find what I really needed— radical queers, runaways, dropouts, anarchists, vegans, addicts, incest survivors, freaks, sluts, whores, and direct action activists trying desperately to piece together a culture of resistance. Soon after arriving in San Francisco, I went to an anti-Bush protest where I brought a sign that said "Break Down the American First Family," and maybe something using the word "assassinate," which didn't go over well with the Secret Service. I was detained for several hours in a Lincoln Town Car with tinted windows — hello FBI file. This was the early '90s in San Francisco, and everywhere queers were dying of AIDS and drug addiction and suicide, but also there was an oppositional queer culture that I could finally grasp, become a part of, hold onto. For me that culture centered around ACT UP, the AIDS Coalition to Unleash Power. ACT UP meant fighting AIDS because everyone was dying, and it also meant making connections — between government neglect of people with AIDS and structural homophobia and racism; between the ever-increasing military budget and the lack of funding for healthcare; between misogyny and the absence of resources for women with AIDS; between the war on drugs and the abandonment of HIV-positive drug addicts and prisoners.

In 1993, I went with ACT UP to the March on Washington for Lesbian, Gay and Bisexual Rights (transgender inclusion was not yet on the table). ACT UP was planning a mass civil disobedience for universal healthcare at the Capitol, but, unlike at past national mobilizations, only several dozen people joined us in getting arrested. Our action took place on the same weekend as the largest gay march in history, which struck me as a sea of uniformity — white gays in white T-shirts applying for Community Spirit credit cards and rallying for the newly-elected President Clinton to follow through on his campaign promise to allow gays to openly serve in the US military. I had never seen anything like it — a million gay people, on the streets of the city where I grew up feeling alone, broken, hopeless for any possibility of self-expression. A million gay people, gathered together to fight for inclusion in the most blatant institution of US imperialism.

A day or two later, after the gay tide had subsided and no change was noticeable on DC streets except for piles of trash, I was making out with the person who would become my first boyfriend, outside the 24-hour restaurant where I used to go late at night in high school. Two white frat types came right up to us and said: what are you doing? Kissing, I said, and went back to it. They sprayed something directly into my eyes from a few inches away, and all I could feel was a searing pain like my whole face was on fire — when I went inside the restaurant to splash cold water on my face it looked like my skin was covered in red spray paint. The manager or someone told me to take this outside. Eventually I got a cab to the hospital, where they said it was pepper spray, and they pumped saline into my eyes for close to an hour, to make sure that I didn't lose my vision. The next day I met my parents for dinner, who unwittingly echoed the gay movement when they asked: why do you have to be so overt?

Getting bashed right after the March on Washington cemented my feelings that the assimilationist gay agenda would never make visible queers safer. In fact, by trumpeting a masculinist, pro-military agenda the gay establishment makes poor people all over the world more vulnerable to U.S. military aggression. It also creates value where there is none, rejecting decades of left opposition to the U.S. military in favor of the smiling, happy, proud, and pumped-up face of the new gay patriot.

It is no coincidence that the obsession with gay inclusion in the U.S. military emerged from the AIDS crisis. In the late-'80s and early-'90s, facing the deaths of lovers, friends, and sometimes entire social networks due not just to a new disease, but the old diseases of government neglect and structural homophobia, queers built systems of care that were breathtaking in their immediacy, shared vision, intimacy, and effectiveness. Out of rage and hopelessness came not just the brilliance of ACT UP, but a generation of incendiary art and brave visions for community-building.

As a 19-year-old queer activist surrounded by grieving, loneliness, desperation and visionary world-making in 1993, I'll admit that I held some hope that universal healthcare might become a central issue for queer struggle. What could have built more beautiful and far-reaching alliances, what could have held a greater impact not just for queers, but for everyone in this country? My hopes for a broad struggle based on universal needs were dashed at the March on Washington, which felt more like a circuit party than a protest: a circuit party with a military theme. Except that this wasn't just drug-fueled bacchanalia or straight-acting role play — brushing aside the ashes of dead lovers, the gay movement battled for the right to do its own killing.

The effects of this new gay militarism can be seen in all segments of the movement now pronounced "LGBT." As marriage entered the fray as the dominant gay issue, the stars and stripes began to eclipse even the empty

5

symbolism of the sweatshop-produced nylon rainbow flag: gay (and "gay-friendly") people everywhere draped themselves in the U.S. flag at virtually every pro-marriage demonstration as the U.S. obliterated Iraq and Afghanistan, occupied Haiti, and funded the Israeli war on the Palestinians. Then there's the law-and-order message intrinsic to the fight for hate crimes legislation — that's right, the way to keep queer people safe is to put more power in the hands of a notoriously racist, classist, misogynist, homophobic and transphobic system, right? Kill those criminals twice, and then they won't be around to engage in more violence.

But the effects of the pro-military gay agenda do not end there. Corporate-friendly, media-savvy gay lobbying groups have developed a stranglehold on popular representations of what it means to be queer, making sure that everyone knows that the only way to be "pro-LGBT" is to support marriage "equality," military inclusion, and hate crimes legislation. Maybe with the rest of our time we can fight for ordination into the priesthood while demanding gay and lesbian parental rights without talking about autonomy for children. Even when these gays in suits do talk about issues that matter, like nondiscrimination in housing or employment, the rhetoric prioritizes the most privileged while fucking over everyone else — sure, it's a great idea to protect people who already have housing or jobs, but what about the rest of us?

Unfortunately, the left is complicit in this silencing agenda. The left has never done its work to address structural homophobia, so now that the gays have Ellen (and Rachel Maddow!), left pundits are eager to prove themselves as gay-friendly as your average P-FLAG soccer mom. And so, ironically, what we see, over and over, are conservative gay media hacks welcome in allegedly liberal, progressive, and even radical media venues, spouting off on the importance of gays in the military on antiwar programs, talking about marriage inclusion with straight radio hosts who are veterans of the '60s and made the conscious political choice never to get married, and foaming at the mouth about making anti-gay or anti-trans murderers pay for their crimes in the same pages where the injustices of the prison industrial complex are highlighted.

Occasionally a queer critique of the gay establishment appears on the left (including some of the pieces reprinted in this book). In 2010, I had the rare opportunity to appear on Democracy Now, a show I watch pretty much every day, to debate Lieutenant Dan Choi, a cover model for patriotic gays everywhere. On the show, he declared, with rare clarity: "War is a force that gives us meaning."

What, exactly, is the meaning of the U.S. obliterating Iraq, Afghanistan, and Pakistan? What is the meaning of soldiers pressing buttons in Nevada to destroy villages halfway around the world? What is the meaning of U.S. soldiers in Afghanistan establishing a "kill team" in order to murder innocent civilians, pose for photographs with the dead bodies, and cut off fingers as souvenirs? The U.S. is involved in overt and covert wars all over the world, in order to plunder indigenous resources for corporate profit. And the meaning of the fight for gays in the military is that the gay establishment will do anything to become part of the status quo. But nothing could be more hypocritical than a movement centering around the right to go abroad to kill people and get away with it. If that is a "civil rights" struggle, as we are led to believe, there is a problem with civil rights.

On September 20, 2011, the ban on gay soldiers serving openly in the U.S. military ended, and over 100 celebrations were planned in cities across the U.S. and around the world. How many antiwar demonstrations were planned on the same day? What if 18 years of fighting for gays in the military were spent fighting against the U.S. military?

This book archives queer challenges to the militarization of gay identity, exposing the sad trajectory from gay liberation to gay assimilation. These essays spotlight the U.S. military's role in enforcing heterosexual norms and white supremacy, and ask what is lost when so much energy, attention, and financial resources are misdirected in the service of empire. Support for the U.S. military in this day and age always comes at the cost of social programs and social justice. A movement that should be about gender, sexual, social, political and cultural self-determination, not just for queers in this country, but for everyone in this country and around the world is instead centered around accessing dominant systems of oppression. As a queer teenager growing up in an abusive family and a homophobic world, I believed there were people like me but I didn't believe that I would ever find them. When I rejected the world that had made me — its homophobia, transphobia, racism, classism, misogyny, ableism, and all other forms of oppression and hierarchy, I never imagined there was a parallel violence on the other side of coming out, a gay establishment that believed in the right to fight in unjust wars. As long as war is a force that gives us meaning, there will never be hope for meaning anything else.

This piece originally appeared on Queers for Economic Justice's website (www.q4ej.org) on December 22, 2010, on the occasion of President Obama's repeal of DADT.

A Military Job Is Not Economic Justice: QEJ Statement on DADT
Kenyon Farrow for QEJ

In just a few moments President Obama is scheduled to sign the repeal of the Don't Ask, Don't Tell (DADT) policy which, in theory, will allow for gay and lesbian members of the military to serve without being in the closet.

Queers for Economic Justice staff and constituents have all met people in the LGBT movement who have said to us that the DADT repeal is an economic justice victory, since many poor and working-class LGBT people join the military to have access to better jobs, and because the military is the nation's largest employer, QEJ should be joining in the victory dance.

But QEJ believes military service is not economic justice, and it is immoral that the military is the nation's de facto jobs program for poor and working-class people. Since QEJ organizes LGBTQ homeless people in New York City, we wanted to remind the LGBT community and progressive anti-war allies that militarism and war profiteering do not serve the interests of LGBT people. Here's how:

1) The National Coalition for Homeless Veterans reports that about one-third of all homeless people in the U.S. are veterans, but about 1.5 million more veterans are at risk of homelessness "due to poverty, lack of support networks, and dismal living conditions in overcrowded or substandard housing." They also report that 56% of homeless veterans are Black or Latino.

2) Some studies also show that one in four veterans becomes disabled as a result of physical violence or emotional trauma of war. There are currently 30,000 disabled veterans from the wars in Iraq and Afghanistan.

3) Rape and sexual violence are very common occurrences for women in the military, and the ACLU is currently suing the Pentagon to get the real numbers on reported incidences.

4) Half of the U.S. budget in 2009 was made up of military spending, including current expenditures, veterans' benefits and the portion of the national debt caused by military costs, according to the War Resisters' League. That is more than the U.S. spent on Health & Human Services, Social Security Administration, Housing and Urban Development and the Department of Education combined. Wouldn't more social safety net spending help the millions of queers who can barely make ends meet?

In short, military service is not economic justice.

Furthermore, QEJ understands that there are LGBTQ people in other parts of the world, particularly Iraq and Afghanistan, who have been killed, traumatized, or made disabled directly as a result of the recent U.S.-led wars, or who have become vulnerable targets by fundamentalist backlashes to US imperialism. We stand in solidarity with other LGBTQ people around the globe, and do not condone violence against them or their home countries so that "our gays" have the "right" to serve openly in the military.

This piece originally appeared online at CounterPunch.org on February 10, 2010.

Don't Ask, Don't Tell, Don't Serve
Cecilia Cissell Lucas

"Don't Ask, Don't Tell" is bad policy. It encourages deceit and, specifically, staying in the closet, which contributes to internalized as well as public homophobia, thus perpetuating discrimination and violence against LGBT people. Banning gay people from serving in the military, however, is something I support. Not because I'm anti-gay, nope, I'm one of those queer folks myself. I'm also a woman and would support a law against women serving in the military. Not because I think women are less capable. I would support laws against any group of people serving in the military: people of color, tall people, people between the ages of 25 and 53, white men, poor people, people who have children, people who vote for Democrats — however you draw the boundaries of a group, I would support a law banning them from military service. Because I support outlawing the military. And until that has happened, I support downsizing it by any means necessary, including, in this one particular arena, sacrificing civil rights in the interest of human rights.

Civil rights would dictate that if a military exists, everyone, regardless of race, gender, sexuality, class or religion, should have an equal opportunity to serve in it. But human rights dictate otherwise. Human rights do not support the equal right of everyone to kill. They support the right of everyone NOT to be killed, occupied and exploited — another key function militaries carry out. As such, human rights are anti-military by nature.

I want to be clear that I'm not one of those knee-jerk anti-soldier types. I grew up in a military family, spent many years bagging groceries in an army commissary, and lots of time on military bases — the point is, as individuals, military personnel are as diverse a group of people as are academics or artists, the other two groups of people I've spent a lot of time around. Racism, sexism, homophobia, poverty-by-design — these problems are institutionalized throughout this country and you'll find people who accept the status quo as well as those fighting the long slow battle against injustice in all institutions, including the branches of the military. What makes the military unique is not the individuals in uniform but the fact that their job description, in the final instance, is to kill people. Legally and explicitly. Killing is not the exclusive or even the most frequent activity performed, but it is the ultimate threat, the ultimate purpose of having armed forces.

It's sad that advocating for the outlawing of the military is widely seen as naïve and utopian: after all, there are threats out there and without a military we would be defenseless. It's ironic that many who make that argument in support of the military also consider themselves Christians. Even though, to my understanding, being a Christian means "walking the Jesus path." And didn't Jesus refuse to use arms (or to let family or friends do so on his behalf) even in self-defense, even though that commitment resulted in his death? When it comes down to it, though, I'm not as principled as Jesus. I support the use of violence in slave uprisings and anti-colonial movements. I imagine that I would kill someone whom I witnessed in the act of attempting to kill, torture or rape others or myself, if I had the means and if that were the only way to stop that act from happening. But what all of those situations have in common reflect a way in which the U.S. military is rarely used: to stop brutality as it is happening.

Queerness, broadly speaking, is a challenge to mainstream common sense. Why should we buy into the mantra of it being necessary to have a military? Or of American lives being so much more worthy than the lives of others that "collateral damage" in the course of preventing a possible attack on the U.S. is acceptable? Let's take the Orwellian factor out of the term "defense" and restore that word to its actual meaning: let's create a defense force that is ready to respond and is only utilized when actual attacks are in-progress. Not to enforce the unequal trade policies from which we benefit, not to enforce the installment or removal of politicians to better serve U.S. interests, not to prevent attacks on the U.S. And certainly not to attack people who are not actively killing, enslaving, colonizing, or torturing anyone. You can shoot down the plane as it is heading for the World Trade Center, but not bomb targets you suspect of harboring terrorists planning future attacks. Yes, that means risking the possible death of innocent Americans in a future attack. But the alternative is to guarantee the death of innocent non-Americans based on conjecture.

There is a lot of talk about the military "protecting" Americans. Frankly, a much better job of that will be done if the funds diverted from scaling back the military to an actual defense force are invested in universal health care, education, job creation, living wage legislation, cancer research, and the like. Eradicating poverty and ensuring health care will save far more lives every year than so-called "national security." There are far too many Americans who do, indeed, lead insecure lives. But terrorism is the least cause of their condition — the more significant threats are domestic policies that see their lives as acceptable collateral damage to an increasingly unregulated capitalism of every man for himself. In fact, the majority of young people who join the military do so out of their own sense of insecurity and a desire to make a difference in the world. They cite the military as the only option they see to afford college and/or to receive a steady paycheck, and as a source of meaningful work. Propaganda ensures that they can pursue this path without going insane, by being led to believe that they are heroes, nobly serving their country. But I believe that our country (not to mention many other places in the world) is actually being done a grave disservice by sacrificing such a large portion of our material and human resources to the military. And it is a tragedy that so many young people's desires to do good are preyed upon, manipulated through fear-mongering nationalist ideology, and diverted into the destruction of lives, the devastation of the planet, and the perpetuation of inequality.

Instead of fighting for the right to serve in the military, let's fight for the right of military service being prohibited. To increase our national security. And for the protection of all our human rights, globally.

*   *   *

Afterthought

It is tricky to write an essay that accepts discrimination as a means to an end. In what remains a homophobic, racist, sexist society, I fear enabling a slippery slope of arguments for identity-based discrimination. Although, of course, the entire notion of citizens who are "protected" by a military discriminates against people based on the identity factor of nationality. Hence my point about human rights trumping civil rights. My argument that we should be fighting against, not for, gay people's inclusion in the military is not actually about gay people at all. Nor is it about wanting others to do our dirty work for us. As I said, I think everyone should be banned from military service. But if the goal is demilitarization, fighting for even more people to have the right to join the military makes no sense. There are plenty of other civil rights denied gay people for which we still need to fight — civil rights that do not trample on others' human rights.

This piece originally appeared in issue 12 of the Montreal-based online magazine No More Potlucks (nomorepotlucks.org).

Rage, or the Lack Thereof

Yasmin Nair

A man stands chained to a fence, his face carefully composed in a look that can only be described as telegenic martyrdom. He is wearing a camouflage military uniform, and a black beret. The fence, it turns out, is the one around the White House. The man's name is Dan Choi, it is March 2010, and he is set to become a symbol of all the contradictions of the new political rage in the United States.

What was Dan Choi so angry about in March — and again in April — of 2010? My leftist, anti-war heart beats more quickly at such a sight because I always imagine that the soldier in question is about to launch into a critique of the U.S war machine: "With this act, I declare the end of my allegiance to the project of death and destruction carried out by our country." Or some such thing. You get the point.

So it was a disappointment to me to learn that Choi was protesting the fact that he, a gay soldier discharged under the U.S. military's "Don't Ask, Don't Tell" policy, was protesting his ouster and demanding to be let back in. Wait. "What was that again?" you ask. A man enters an institution, a man is unfairly ejected after it is discovered that he is gay, thus revealing, we must assume, said institution to be deeply flawed and even dangerous. And then the man demands to be let back in. If the definition of insanity is doing the same thing over and over again…is Dan Choi insane?

No, to the best of my knowledge, but he has frequently taken on the mantle of martyrdom, often comparing himself to historical figures like Martin Luther King and Mahatma Gandhi, as in an interview with *Newsweek* shortly after his first protest.[1] In the same interview, he spoke grandly against the stereotype of West Point graduates like him as a privileged people[2]: "We are tired of being stereotyped as privileged, bourgeois elites. Is someone willing to give up their career, their relationships with powerful people, their Rolodex, or their parents' love to stand up for who they are? I'm giving up my military rank, my unit—which to me is a family—my veterans' benefits, my health care, so what are you willing to sacrifice?"

One might be excused for being stunned into (temporary) silence at the sheer audacity of this statement. To date, over 50 million in the U.S. are without health insurance. Millions work without benefits or have seen a sizable cut in them. Medical costs constitute the leading cause of bankruptcy in the country. According to one report, citing a Harvard study, "62% of all personal bankruptcies in the U.S. in 2007 were caused by health problems — and 78% of those filers had insurance."[3] Given all this, it is hard to be admonished by a member of the ever-shrinking elite with benefits when one has none to sacrifice. As for his question about whether or not the rest of us are willing to give up "relationships with powerful people": he has, I think, a great many of us — who don't have such relationships in the first place — stumped.

As if his statement about who has privilege and who does not was not startling enough, Choi went on to speak of his experience in Iraq when the reporter asked him what it was like to be in jail: "I've detained people in Iraq, I've read them their rights, and I've applied handcuffs and zip ties. I've talked with people in Arabic who've just been arrested. I know what it means to arrest someone for my country's mission. But I've never been incarcerated, and for something that I thought was not my country's mission. I know my country's mission is not to make an entire group of people into second-class citizens."

This last sentence should give pause to anyone who knows anything of what goes on in Iraq and Afghanistan, or has even heard of the infamous Abu Ghraib photographs.

As expected, much of the gay press and community have held up Choi as their martyr. If there is dissension around him, it comes not from an examination of what his politics might mean but what they look like. While GetEqual, the group behind Choi, proclaims that it is "radical" for supposedly daring to engage in tactics like those used by Choi, the more conservative Human Rights Campaign (HRC), with a $35 million budget, focuses on expensive fundraisers and lobbying politicians in D.C., where the organization is based. Broadly speaking, the mainstream LGBT community in the U.S. advances an agenda whose ideology ranges from the right to the center of right. Issues like marriage, DADT, and hate crimes legislation take up the economic and political capital of the "community" while matters like the homelessness of queer youth or the drop in AIDS funding are routinely set aside with the explanation that the first three will take care of the rest. GetEqual, HRC, and GOProud simply want the status quo—in the form of marriage and the rest — to be expanded to gays and lesbians. None of their activism, in any form, challenges the hierarchy established by marriage, for instance.

Which is to say: conservative issues like marriage, DADT, and hate crimes legislation are the emphasis in the mainstream gay community, and the only differences between such groups lie in the styles of the advocacy they engage in, not the content. Yet a recent Washington Post article about the gay rights movement declared that HRC was on the left of the gay community and GOProud, the gay Republican group, was on the right. The fact that both groups are fighting for exactly the same thing did not seem to have occurred to the reporter.

But therein lies the fundamental problem with the Left in the U.S.: its utter inability to separate itself from conservatives and liberals who, after all, merely want more of the same. When it comes to defining who is left and who is right, the distinctions come down to style, not ideology. Under these circumstances, it is no surprise that Choi should emerge as the brave and angry martyr who has had enough and will risk such things as "relationships to important people." And he is regarded as such even by those on the left, like Amy Goodman, the popular host of the progressive television and radio show Democracy Now, who should know better.

Amy Goodman is as popular as she is among lefties and liberals because she is often one of the few anti-war voices of reason on the radio. But Goodman has had Dan Choi on Democracy Now a few times and has never once criticized his fervent pro-war and pro-U.S. imperialist rhetoric. Not only that, she has gone so far as to pen not one but two op-eds, one of them titled "Lt. Choi Won't Lie for His Country," in which she repeated some of what he said to during a 2009 interview: "Choi got a message from an Iraqi doctor whose hospital Choi helped to rebuild while he was there. He said the doctor is 'in South Baghdad right now. And he's seen some of the Internet, YouTube and CNN interviews and other appearances, and he said: 'Brother, I know that you're gay, but you're still my brother, and you're my friend. And if your country, that sent you to my country, if America, that sent you to Iraq, will discharge you such that you can't get medical benefits, you can come to my hospital any day. You can come in, and I will give you treatment.'" More recently, Choi was on Democracy Now, in a debate with the queer radical anti-war activist Mattilda Bernstein Sycamore, and said, "…war is a force that gives us meaning. War is a force that teaches us lessons of humanity and allows us to realize something about our society and teaches us the lessons that we probably should have learned before we went to war." Neither Goodman nor Juan Gonzalez, her co-host, blinked an eye. Goodman has not simply featured Choi's views on her show, she has explicitly endorsed them in her op-eds outside her role as show co-host.

Within today's left, or what passes for the same, it is actually possible to have someone like Goodman, who has spent many hours among commentators critiquing the devastation caused to Iraq, listen to Choi talk about "rebuilding" a country that he is helping to bomb and destroy, without a single question about his politics. In this case, identity — and its efflorescence under a neoliberal war — becomes the excuse for war and it erases the possibility of a critique of Choi's ideology. Even further, the war on Iraq becomes a staging ground for Chois's personal dramas, a backdrop to the possibility of a doomed romance. As Mattilda Bernstein Sycamore puts it, "How many Iraqis died in order for him to express the 'truth of who I am?' What about the truth of the war?…Did you hear that? He's not worried about dying in an atrocious war, or killing innocent civilians, but about whether his boyfriend will be notified."[4]

Choi's anger at having been expelled from the military and his on-the-surface radical tactics are symptomatic of the failure of the Left in the U.S to mobilize for the things that matter, like health care, leaving the political arena wide open for the likes of gay soldiers to angrily demand that they should be allowed to fight unjust wars. Modern times have rarely been worse in the United States, and yet, all over, there is anger about maintaining the status quo instead of meaningful change. Hence the growth of the Tea Party and its deployment of anger, much of it foolish and misplaced, as in the signs that read, "Keep the government out of my Medicare [the government's form of health care for the elderly]."

In the wake of such struggles, what happens to the efforts of those who do fight for actual change?

Here in Chicago, I am a member of Gender JUST (GJ), a largely youth-led organization that has, for nearly two years, successfully fought for a Chicago Public Schools (CPS) to institute a grievance process that would make it easier for students to report harassment and bullying. The current CEO of CPS, Ron Huberman is an out gay man with a partner and an adopted infant. For nearly two years, Huberman stalled on meeting with GJ and acting upon his promise to help make schools safer for youth, particularly queer youth, despite public promises to do so. Finally, the group decided to enact the kind of tactics long employed by direct action groups: it showed up at Huberman's public appearances and even went to his house with a basket of cookies and testimonials from youth who had been harassed and bullied. Eventually, after a series of such escalations, Huberman agreed to institute a grievance process.

In the wake of the protest outside his house, we were told by some that they were troubled or even offended by the fact that GJ would actually show up at the house — where his child was. It was as if GJ had shown up and threatened to take away the infant, or had thrown stones at it. As Sam Finkelstein, one of the lead organizers, put it to me, "Why is no one thinking of the children and youth who suffer daily harassment and agony simply for going to school?" Implicit in the criticism of the actions was the idea that Huberman's private residence should be invulnerable and that GJ had committed a major social infraction by daring to go to his house. This kind of logic is typical of protests in the U.S. where dissent and protest have been nearly squelched by endlessly minute and refined bureaucratic efforts, via the process of having to ask for permits for every action or the constant admonition, during protests, to keep moving and stay on the sidewalk, instead of taking over the streets.

The students of Chicago's public schools study in the nation's most militarized school district; its largely minority and often poor population is constantly targeted by the U.S. army for recruitment. Over the years, there has been admirable resistance to such militarization from many local educators on the left and groups like Gender JUST which have consistently been critical of such developments. Those criticizing GJ for its tactics failed to make the connections between Huberman's supposed imperviousness to protest while inside his home, and the extreme vulnerability of students within school walls.

Our rage, the productive sort which might actually demand change, is constantly being curtailed either by convenient distinctions between private and public or by a public discourse which fails to see the contradictions in a gay soldier who considers himself a second-class citizen of the U.S. while handcuffing Iraqis. Rage appears in stylistic flourishes, as in the Tea Party protests where citizens rant and rave about policies about which they have little understanding or by soldiers demanding "fair" treatment in an institution that is fundamentally unfair to the rest of the world.

Rage has dissipated into conciliation and a call for the status quo.

References

[1] http://www.newsweek.com/2010/03/21/this-is-my-mission.html

[2] Choi was responding to criticisms that elite military personnel like him, who graduate from institutions like West Point and choose to enter the military with specialized skills, are different from the much poorer young Latino/a or African American youth aggressively recruited by the army with the explicit promise of social mobility. The U.S. military still boasts of the G.I. Bill of 1944 as the best example of how it provides college or vocational education for returning veterans, along with various loans for homes and businesses. But today, with military service being largely voluntary, the military must rely on aggressive and even duplicitous forms of recruitment. In its advertising, it shamelessly deploys narratives about troubled youth of color within single-mother households who need the discipline, targeting them as ideal candidates for "discipline" on its visits to high schools (where it is allowed to enter for recruitment purposes); it even goes so far as to recruit undocumented youth with the false promise of eventual citizenship. Today, the military depends on a two-tier system for recruitment: elite soldiers like Choi, who enter voluntarily, and the economically and politically disenfranchised who join out of desperation.

[3]http://www.businessweek.com/bwdaily/dnflash/content/jun2009/db2009064_666715.htm?campaign_id=rss_daily

[4]http://www.bilerico.com/2010/08/a_fine_romance_democracy_nows_amy_goodman_and_lieu.php

This piece was originally published on February 25, 2009 in the Chicago based LGBT paper, Windy City Times.

Queer Eyes on What Prize? Ending DADT
Erica Meiners & Therese Quinn

So, we've heard that Barack Obama is going to repeal the Don't Ask, Don't Tell policy that prohibits gays and lesbians from serving openly in the military. As two queer teachers that have been working hard to arrest the militarism of education in Chicago — a public high school for every branch of the military, and two for the army (and not one of these with a Gay Straight Alliance for students), and over 10,000 youth from 6th to 12th grade participating in some form of military program in their public schools — we are not leaping with joy at this rumor. Our reluctance has our allies scratching their heads:

"Isn't this what you want?"

"Equal right to fight!"

"What a success for the gay rights movement!"

"I guess this solves the discrimination problem in military public schools, then."

"Gay kids can join up!"

Sure, we think uniforms are hot, but this — permitting out lesbians and gay men to enlist — was never the purpose of gay liberation, a movement aiming as tenaciously at peace as equal rights.

And for us, it's clear that overturning Don't Ask, Don't Tell (DADT) won't begin to address the public policy catastrophe of turning over our public schools, and some of our nation's poorest youth, to the military.

We argue that the system of public education should remain a civilian system. This statement rests on three proposals. First, adults may choose to enlist; youth cannot. Next, schools should educate students for the broadest possibilities and choices; the military narrowly aims to prepare recruits. And last, schools should protect young people and nurture peace; but the military is contagiously violent. From the ugly revelations of Abu Ghraib, and the rash of sexual assaults on military women by men in service, to many veterans' post-service violence turned both inward and outward — its legacy of brutality is so vast that the Department of Defense might more aptly be called the Department of Destruction.

This proposed repeal, far from any big win, offers queers an important opportunity to think about our strategies and goals. Let's not unfurl our victory banner too quickly; instead, we should keep our queer eyes, and organizing, focused on the real prize: social justice.

Yes, gays, lesbians and transgendered folks are discriminated against and excluded from full participation in our society and its institutions, including schools (read any report about rates of violence against gay students or employment discrimination for out queer or non-gendering conforming school staff), military (DADT — enough said?), families (remember the 57% majority that passed the 2008 gay adoption ban in Arkansas) and religion (many religious colleges and universities ban homosexual students, staff, and faculty — legally!) .

Add to this list the ease with which otherwise smart people, including President Obama, reserve marriage and all its attendant privileges for "one man and one woman" while also claiming they are "ferocious" defenders of gay rights — that's a fairly self-serving stance, isn't it? Yes, gays and lesbians still have a long way to go toward achieving... let's just call it "fully human status" in the United States.

The push to repeal DADT is, on the one hand, a no-brainer — all people should have all rights, right?

But this proposal can also be understood, and it is by us, as an attempt to remap what our social justice goals, as queers, should be — not the right to privacy and the right to public life, and certainly not the right to live lives free from our nation's ever-present militarism and never-ending war. Instead, lesbians, gays, transgendered and bisexuals are encouraged to forget our historical places at the helm of social justice thinking and labor (to mention just a few, Jane Addams, Bayard Rustin, Barbara Jordan, and of course, Harvey Milk), constrict our vision and dreams, and just be happy for an opportunity to participate in a military that depends on poverty and permanent war to keep enlistment high.

Let's forget repealing DADT and cut right to the chase: Repeal the Department of Defense. What about establishing a Department of Peace, as Dennis Kucinich has already proposed? Let's pair that with bear brigades tossing pink batons (and, of course, an annual teddy bear picnic). Or, we can take up the mermaid parade as an organizing celebration, with its dress-up and float creation. Either of these fanciful, and very queer, forms would allow us all to play and create together, and each seems a better activity for a school to take up that pretend soldiering.

Then let's organize for some real social justice goals.

For starters, let's demand universal healthcare, affordable housing, and meaningful living wage employment that supports flourishing, not merely subsisting, lives, for all.

We know we don't need 6th or 12th graders wearing military uniforms, marching with wooden guns on public school grounds. We don't need twelve year olds parsing military ranks or plotting battles. However, we could use more teens painting murals, stitching gowns, and writing code and lyrics. In short, we don't need child soldiers, but we could use more young artists.

A public school system that teaches peace and art, with fiercely equal opportunities for all students. We can see it now: painting classes, soccer clubs, computer gaming classes, drum-kits, comprehensive sexuality education, and musical theatre in every school. That's so excellently queer, and so very just.

*This piece originally appeared on Tamara K. Nopper's blog
(bandung1955.wordpress.com) on September 19, 2010.*

Why I Oppose Repealing DADT & Passage of the DREAM Act

Tamara K. Nopper

One of the first books I read about Asian American
feminism was the anthology *Dragon Ladies: Asian American
Feminists Breathe Fire*. In one of the essays, author Juliana
Pegues describes scenes from a "radical Asian women's
movement."   One such scene involves lesbian and
bisexual Asian and Pacific Islanders marching at Gay
Pride with signs reading "Gay white soldiers in Asia? Not
my liberation!" and "ends with the absence of all soldiers,
gay and straight, from any imperialist army."

Although it has been over a decade since I read this
passage, I return to this "scene" as I watch far too many
liberals and progressives praise the possible repeal of
Don't Ask, Don't Tell (DADT) as well as the possible
passage of the DREAM Act (Development, Relief, and
Education for Alien Minors Act).

In some ways, I understand why people are supportive of
such gestures. The idea that certain identities and status

categories, such as gay or lesbian or (undocumented) immigrants are either outlawed or treated as social problems has rightfully generated a great deal of sympathy. And the very real ways that people experience marginalization or discrimination — ranging from a lack of certain rights to violence, including death — certainly indicates that solutions are needed. Further, far too many non-whites have experienced disproportionate disadvantages, surveillance, and discipline from both DADT and anti-immigrant legislation. For example, Black women, some of whom are not lesbians, have been disproportionately discharged from the U.S. military under DADT. And anti-immigrant legislation, policing measures, and vigilante xenophobic racism is motivated by and reinforces white supremacy and white nationalism.

Yet both the repeal of DADT and the passage of the DREAM Act will increase the size and power of the U.S. military and the Department of Defense, which is already the largest U.S. employer. Repealing DADT will make it easier for gays and lesbians to openly serve and the Dream Act in its present incarnation may provide a pathway to legal residency and possibly citizenship for some undocumented immigrant young people if they serve two years in the U.S. military or spend an equal amount of time in college.

Unsurprisingly, the latter, being pushed by Democrats, is getting support from "many with close ties to the military and higher education." As the *Wall Street Times* reports:

> "Pentagon officials support the Dream Act. In its strategic plan for fiscal years 2010-2012, the Office of the Under Secretary of Defense for Personnel and Readiness cited the Dream Act as

a 'smart' way to attract quality recruits to the all-volunteer force...

'Passage of the Dream Act would be extremely beneficial to the U.S. military and the country as a whole,' said Margaret Stock, a retired West Point professor who studies immigrants in the military. She said it made 'perfect' sense to attach it to the defense-authorization bill.

Louis Caldera, secretary of the Army under President Bill Clinton, said that as they struggled to meet recruiting goals, 'recruiters at stations were telling me it would be extremely valuable for these patriotic people to be allowed to serve our country.'"

Additionally, in a 2009 Department of Defense strategic plan report, the second strategic goal, "Shape and maintain a mission-ready All Volunteer Force," lists the DREAM Act as a possible recruitment tool under one of the "performance objectives":

"Recruit the All-Volunteer Force by finding smart ways to sustain quality assurance even as we expand markets to fill manning at controlled costs as demonstrated by achieving quarterly recruiting quality and quantity goals, and through expansion of the Military Accessions Vital to the National Interest (MAVNI) program and the once-medically restricted populations, as well as the DREAM initiative."

What concerns me is that far too many liberals and progressives, including those who serve as professional commentators on cable news and/or progressive publications (and some with a seemingly deep affinity for the Democratic Party) have been praising the passage of the DREAM Act. Unsurprising is that many of the same people support the repeal of DADT. While a sincere concern about discrimination may unite both gestures, so too does a lack of critical perspective regarding the U.S. military as one of the main vehicles in the expansion and enforcement of U.S. imperialism, heterosexuality, white supremacy, capitalism, patriarchy, and repression against political dissent and people's movements in the United States and abroad. Far too many liberals and progressives, including those critical of policies or the squashing of political dissent, take an ambivalent stance on the U.S. military. It is unclear what makes some of these folks unwilling to openly oppose the military state. Perhaps it's easier than dealing with the backlash from a variety of people, including the many people of color and/or women who are now building long-term careers in the military. Or maybe it's more amenable to building careers as pundits in both corporate and progressive media, both of which may be critical of some defense spending or "wasted" (read unsuccessful) military efforts but not necessarily of U.S. militarism.

Whatever the case, the inclusion of more gays and lesbians and/or undocumented immigrant youth in the U.S. military is not an ethical project given that both gestures are willing to have our communities serve as mercenaries in exchange for certain rights, some of which are never fully guaranteed in a homophobic and white supremacist country. Nor is it pragmatic. By supporting the diversification of the U.S. military we undermine radical democratic possibilities by giving the military state more people, many of whom will ultimately die in combat or develop PTSD and health issues and/or continue nurturing long-term relationships with the U.S. military, including a political affinity with its culture and goals. We will also have a more difficult time challenging projects of privatization, the incurring of huge amounts of debt, and the erosion of rights and protections in other countries — efforts buttressed by the threat of military action— which ultimately affects people in the United States.

Of course I am not the first person to raise these concerns. There are gay, lesbian, bisexual, and transgender folks, many of them non-white and non-middle class, who promote a queer politic that challenges the heteronormative desires of mainstream movements, including that pushed by some LGBT organizations and their purported "allies" within the Democratic party and heteronormative people of color organizations. Some of these folks organize for better economic opportunities, access to housing, and safer existences in the civilian sector for poor and working-class LGBTs. And some also openly oppose military recruitment or challenge the push for gays and lesbians to (openly) serve in the military by countering with "Don't serve" as a slogan. For example, Cecilia Lucas, who grew up in a military family, writes in a 2010 *CounterPunch* article:

> "Don't Ask, Don't Tell is bad policy. It encourages deceit and, specifically, staying in the closet, which contributes to internalized as well as public homophobia, thus perpetuating discrimination and violence against LGBT people. Banning gay people from serving in the military, however, is something I support. Not because I'm anti-gay, nope, I'm one of those queer folks myself. I'm also a woman and would support a law against women serving in the military. Not because I think women are less capable. I would support laws against any group

of people serving in the military: people of color, tall people, people between the ages of 25 and 53, white men, poor people, people who have children, people who vote for Democrats — however you draw the boundaries of a group, I would support a law banning them from military service. Because I support outlawing the military. And until that has happened, I support downsizing it by any means necessary, including, in this one particular arena, sacrificing civil rights in the interest of human rights...

It is tricky to write an essay that accepts discrimination as a means to an end. In what remains a homophobic, racist, sexist society, I fear enabling a slippery slope of arguments for identity-based discrimination. Although, of course, the entire notion of citizens who are "protected" by a military discriminates against people based on the identity factor of nationality. Hence my point about human rights trumping civil rights. My argument that we should be fighting against, not for, gay people's inclusion in the military is not actually about gay people at all. Nor is it about wanting others to do our dirty work for us. As I said, I think everyone should be banned from military service. But if the goal is demilitarization, fighting for even more people to have the right to join the military makes no sense. There are plenty of other civil rights denied gay people for which we still need to fight — civil rights that do not trample on others' human rights."

As Lucas's comments reveal, opposing LGBT folks from serving openly in the military is not to condone the

38

harassment and unfair surveillance that they experience; nor is it meant to support a culture that suggests they should stay in the closet in the name of military stability and national security. Rather, it is to discourage the attractiveness of military enlistment as well as martial citizenship, a process that provides marginalized groups a "pathway to citizenship" via military service. More, opposition to people serving in the military is also grounded in an understanding that the military negatively impacts practically everyone in the world (including those in the United States), and in particular people of color and/or women and/or gays and lesbians, and not just those who are discriminated against while serving or who are expected to serve as pathways to citizenship or access to education.

Along with folks like Lucas, there are immigrants and their allies challenging us to rethink the possible passage of the DREAM Act because of its pro-military provision and for basically "making a pool of young, bilingual, U.S.-educated, high-achieving students available to the recruiters." Some have withdrawn their support for the current version of the act in objection to its terms. For example, a letter from one such person, Raúl Al-qaraz Ochoa, states:

> "Passage of the DREAM Act would definitely be a step forward in the struggle for Migrant Justice. Yet the politicians in Washington have hijacked this struggle from its original essence and turned dreams into ugly political nightmares. I refuse to be a part of anything that turns us into political pawns of dirty Washington politics. I want my people to be "legalized" but at what cost? We all want it bad. I hear it. I've lived it. But I think it's a matter of

how much we're willing to compromise in order to win victories or crumbs…So if I support the DREAM Act, does this mean I am okay with our people being used as political pawns? Does this mean that my hands will be smeared with the same bloodshed the U.S. spills all over the world? Does this mean I am okay with blaming my mother and my father for migrating "illegally" to the U.S.? Am I willing to surrender to all that in exchange for a benefit? Maybe it's easier for me to say that "I can" because I have papers, right? I'd like to think that it's because my political principles will not allow me to do so, regardless of my citizenship status or personal benefit at stake. Strong movements that achieve greater victories are those that stand in solidarity with all oppressed people of the world and never gain access to rights at the expense of other oppressed groups.

I have come to a deeply painful decision: I can no longer in good political conscience support the DREAM Act because the essence of a beautiful dream has been detained by a colonial nightmare seeking to fund and fuel the U.S. empire machine."

Unfortunately, the willingness of folks like Lucas and Al-qaraz Ochoa as well as others to critically engage military diversification or the passage of the DREAM Act given its military provisions have gotten less air time or attention among liberal and progressives actively pushing for both measures. In terms of repealing DADT, it is unfortunately not surprising that the rejection of military inclusion by LGBT folks has gotten minimal attention from professional progressives, some of whom are straight. Too many straight people who profess to be LGBT allies tend to align themselves with the liberal professional wings of LGBT politics given shared bourgeois notions of "respectable" (i.e., not offensive to straight people) gay politics that also promotes a middle-class notion of democracy — and supports the Democratic Party. Additionally, it's more time efficient to find out what professional LGBT organizations think, since they are more likely to have resources to make it easier to learn their agendas without as much effort as learning from those who politically labor in the margins of the margins, given their critical stances toward the political mainstream. Yet given the tendency for many professional progressives to be on the internet and social media sites, it is a bit telling that many have supported DADT without addressing the critical stances of some LGBT folks against the military state that are easily available on the internet. This noticeable lack of engagement raises some questions: Why is it that the straight progressives are more willing to have gays and lesbians serve in the U.S. military (or get married) than, let's say, breaking bread with and seriously considering the political views of LGBT folks who take radical political stances against the military state (as well as engage in non-middle-class aesthetics)? And why do many straight progressives fight for LGBT folks to openly serve in the military — one of the most dangerous employment sites that requires its laborers to kill and control others, including non-whites and/or LGBTs, in the name of empire — but rarely discuss how working-class, poor, and/or of color LGBTs are treated and politically organize for opportunities in the civilian sector job market where they are also expected to remain closeted, subject to homophobic harassment and surveillance, or excluded altogether?

Also concerning is the willingness of many progressives to support the DREAM Act, despite it possibly being tied up to a defense-authorization bill and having support from a diverse group of people united by a commitment to military recruitment. While some support is due to a righteous critique of white supremacy that shapes pathways to citizenship, some (also) support the DREAM Act because it serves as a form of "reparations" for foreign policies and colonialism toward third world or developing countries once called home to many of the immigrant youth or their families targeted by the legislation That is, the famous quote "We're here because you were there" seems to be the underlying mantra of some pushing for the act's passage. Yet if "being there" involved the U.S. military, it is unclear how a resolution to this issue, ethically or pragmatically, calls for immigrant youth to serve for the same U.S. military that devastated, disrupted, undermined, and still controls many of the policies and everyday life of the immigrants' homelands.

Partially to blame for the uncritical support of the DREAM Act are different factions of the immigrant rights movement, as well as funders and some progressive media, that have pushed for an uncritical embrace of the immigrant rights movement among progressives. It is difficult to raise critical views of the (diverse) immigrant rights movement, even when making it clear that one rejects the white supremacy and white nationalism of the right wing (as well as white-run progressive media and progressive institutions, such as some labor unions) without experiencing some backlash from other progressives, particularly people of color. In turn, critical questions about how immigrant rights movements may support, rather than undermine U.S. hegemony or white supremacy, have been taken off the table at most progressive gatherings, large and small. Subsequently, while some may express concern about the DREAM Act being part of a defense-authorization bill, there are probably fewer who will openly take stands against the bill, given the threat of being labeled xenophobic by some progressives unwilling to reject the U.S. military state or interrogate the politics of immigration from an anti-racist and anti-capitalist perspective. In the process, the military may end up getting easier access to immigrant youth who may have difficulty going to college.

As the passage from *Dragon Ladies* shows, some take into account the complexity of identities and political realities as well as maintain oppositional stances against those apparatuses that are largely responsible for the limited choices far too many people have. Many of us are looking for ways to mediate the very real vulnerabilities and lack of job security, as well as forms of social rejection that causes the stress, fear, and physical consequences experienced before and especially during this recession. And given the recent upsurge in explicit gestures of white supremacy and white nationalism as demonstrated by the growing strength of the Tea Party, it may be the most expedient to play up on the shared support of the U.S. military among a broad spectrum of people in order to secure, at least on paper, some basic rights to which straight and/or white people have gotten access. But progressives who support the repeal of DADT and passage of the DREAM Act might instead consider other political possibilities explored by some of those who are the subjects of such policy debates; these folks, some of whom are desperately in need of protection, job security, and safety, encourage us to resist the urge for quick resolutions that ultimately serve to stabilize the military state and instead explore more humane options — for those targeted by DADT and the DREAM Act as well as the rest of the world.

This piece originally appeared online at CommonDreams.org on June 7th 2011.

Bradley Manning: Rich Man's War, Poor (Gay) Man's Fight

Larry Goldsmith

A poor, young gay man from the rural South joins the U.S. Army under pressure from his father, and because it's the only way left to pay for a college education. He is sent to Iraq, where he is tormented by fellow soldiers who entertain themselves watching "war porn" videos of drone and helicopter attacks on civilians. He is accused of leaking documents to Wikileaks and placed in solitary confinement, where he has been held for more than a year awaiting a military trial. The President of the United States, a former Constitutional law professor lately suffering amnesia about the presumption of innocence, declares publicly that "he broke the law." The United Nations Special Rapporteur on Torture, Amnesty International, and the American Civil Liberties Union express grave concern about the conditions of his imprisonment, and the spokesman for the U.S. State Department is forced to resign after calling it "ridiculous and counterproductive and stupid." A letter signed by 295 noted legal scholars charges that his imprisonment violates the Eighth Amendment prohibition of cruel and unusual punishment and the Fifth Amendment guarantee against punishment without trial, and that procedures used on Manning "calculated to disrupt profoundly the senses or the personality" amount to torture.

The National Gay and Lesbian Task Force, the Lambda Legal Defense and Education Fund, and the Human Rights Campaign, having invested millions lobbying for "gays in the military," have no comment. Of course not. Bradley Manning is not that butch patriotic homosexual, so central to the gays-in-the-military campaign, who Defends Democracy and Fights Terrorism with a virility indistinguishable from that of his straight buddies. He is not that pillar of social and economic stability, only incidentally homosexual, who returns home from the front to a respectable profession and a faithful spouse and children.

No, Bradley Manning is a poor, physically slight computer geek with an Oklahoma accent. He is, let us use the word, and not in a negative way, a sissy. Having grown up in a dysfunctional family in a small town in the South, he is that lonely, maladjusted outsider many gay people have been, or are, or recognize, whether we wish to admit it or not. He broke the law, the President says. And he did so — the liberal press implies, trying terribly hard to temper severity with compassion — because he wasn't man enough to deal with the pressure. He did so because he's a sissy and he couldn't put up with the manly rough-and-tumble that is so important to unit cohesion, like that time three of his buddies assaulted him and instead of taking it like a good soldier he peed in his pants. And then of course he was so embarrassed he threw a hissy fit and sent Wikileaks our nation's most closely guarded secrets, like some petulant teenage girl who gets her revenge by spreading gossip. This is, of course, the classic argument about gays and national security — they'll get beat up or blackmailed and reveal our secrets. And NGLTF, Lambda, and HRC, with their impeccably professional media and lobbying campaign, based on the best branding and polls and focus groups that money could buy, have effectively demolished that insidious stereotype.

They have demolished it by abandoning Bradley Manning.

Why was Bradley Manning in the U.S. Army in the first place? Why does anyone join the U.S. Army nowadays? Perhaps a few join out of a sincere if misguided idealism that they are truly going to defend freedom and democracy. But if that were commonly the case, one would expect to see a certain number of the more affluent classes, those who never stop preaching the need to defend democracy and freedom by military means, eager to enlist. There would be at least a few Bush and Cheney children fighting on the bloody ground of Iraq and Afghanistan.

Dick Cheney, of course, famously explained that he declined to fight in Vietnam—and invoked the privilege of the student deferment five times to avoid being drafted—because he "had better things to do." The draft is now a thing of the past, and the vast majority of those in the U.S. military are there precisely because they do not have better things to do. That is to say, there are few other opportunities available. The official national unemployment rate, now at 9.1 percent, masks a rate more than twice that figure for young people generally and more than three times that rate among young black men. Decent jobs are difficult to get, of course, without a college education. The U.S. manages, in the midst of an international economic crisis, to spend half a billion dollars every day on the wars in Iraq, Afghanistan, and Libya, but the federal and state governments have drastically cut funding for education, and public as well as private universities have reacted to funding cuts with astronomical increases in tuition and fees. Publicly-funded financial assistance to poor students is a thing of the past—except as part of a military recruitment package.

Bradley Manning wanted an education. He also wanted to get away from his family and out of his small town. Military recruiters do not spend much time in middle-class neighborhoods. They seek out those like Bradley Manning: poor, isolated teenagers dazzled by the slick brochures, the cool technology, the lofty rhetoric of duty and honor, and the generous promises—or who see right through the hype but know they have no other option. The military does not discriminate solely on the basis of sexual preference. In its recruitment it has always observed the time-honored and deeply discriminatory precept of "Rich man's war, poor man's fight."

This is the club that NGLTF, Lambda, and HRC would have gay people join. Let us leave aside for the moment the question of whether the club is a defender of freedom and democracy or an imperialist killing machine. It is in either case an institution that sends the Bradley Mannings of the world, and not the Dick Cheneys, to be killed or maimed — killing or maiming the Bradley Mannings, and not the Dick Cheneys, on the other side. Whatever collective psychosexual hang-ups or perverse ideological interests have prevented it from openly accepting homosexuals (or, not so long ago, women, or African-Americans in integrated units), it is an institution whose fundamental design is to send poor people to die defending the interests of the affluent.

We did not need Bradley Manning to tell us that the military is an institution in defense of a class society. But his case does uniquely reveal a seldom-acknowledged disjuncture between modern LGBT politics, based as it is on the individualizing concepts of "gay identity" and "equal rights," and the way in which political power continues to be exercised through social relationships of class. It was a complex combination of factors — a lack of economic and educational opportunities, and the absence of a community and culture where he could be himself as a gay man — that led Bradley Manning to where he is now. These factors cannot be separated into the neat, discrete categories of single-issue politics. Organizations like NGLTF, Lambda Legal, and HRC would like to pretend that Bradley Manning's case is not a "gay issue," or worse, remain silent because they know that it is indeed a gay issue, one that threatens to undermine their carefully-crafted plea for admittance to the military. Addressing it as a gay issue would mean looking critically not only at the specific discriminatory policy of the military, but also at the very purpose of the military. It would mean taking a good close look at the patriotic rhetoric of "equal rights" to serve in an "all-volunteer" military, whose purpose is to defend "freedom" and "democracy," where LGBT people can be just as "virile" in carrying out organized killing as their heterosexual counterparts. It would mean considering how such rhetoric hides unpleasant truths about economic domination in our world, understanding how such domination relies on structures of power embedded in social relations of class, race, and gender, and recognizing that these structures cannot be addressed individually, but must be attacked simultaneously.

Organizations like NGLTF, Lambda Legal, and HRC that define "LGBT rights" as a single issue divorced from such considerations abandon the Bradley Mannings of the world not just to psychological torture by Presidential edict, but at the entrances to universities barred to those without money, at the military recruiting stations that have replaced the financial aid offices, and at the bases where soldiers, when not engaged in killing the declared enemy, learn to entertain themselves by bullying each other and watching war porn.

This piece first appeared on Jamal Rashad Jones' personal blog (ordoesitexplode.wordpress.com) on December 22nd 2010.

Why I Won't Be Celebrating the Repeal of DADT: Queer Soldiers are Still Agents of Genocide

Jamal Rashad Jones

So "Don't Ask Don't Tell" is looking like it will be repealed and there will be a party in the Castro. I, for one, am not going to be one of the many queens marching throughout the streets of the Castro with my American flag, fatigues, and pink helmet shining.

It seems almost ironic that the Queer liberation movement (now more aptly called the Gay Rights movement) has done a 180 since its radical inception. If anyone were to look into the rich history of Queer struggle they would, no doubt, come into close contact with the Gay Liberation Front (GLF). This group of radical queer groups, which crystallized around the time of the Stonewall Riots, took its name from the Vietnamese Liberation Front. This show of solidarity, through name, was symbolic of the fact that the GLA took a stance against capitalism, racism, and patriarchy in all their forms.

51

Gay Rights activists now find themselves crying out for marriage equality and inclusion in the military as if these issues are at the core of what it means to be a Queer oppressed in our current society and as if the rash of media-covered teen suicides would not happen if these two barriers could be overcome. They clearly have forgotten or didn't get the memo about the U.S. army being the symbol of Western imperialism and marriage being the backbone of patriarchy. Other issues, such as decent housing, medical treatment, and resistance to police brutality have become things associated with people of color and other groups. Gays have obviously come to a place where these are non-issues in their minds. Queer assimilation is the sinister nature of the State and Capitalism at its finest.

> "The most dangerous creation of any society
> is the man who has nothing to lose."
> - James A. Baldwin

The Queer population, in addition to others in the 60's and 70's, fought against the State and Capitalism, in large part because they had no material connection to the State. Queers found themselves outside of the nuclear family structure and the light of mainstream acceptance. This is why you see the great flight to San Francisco happen; this is why you see San Francisco become a Mecca of all things Gay. A home was needed and a home was found. This home, ironically, is the most symbolic of the radical change that has happened in the Queer population in the last 40-50 years.

The Castro district in San Francisco now stands as the most alienating piece of land to anyone that finds himself or herself not a rich, white, gay male. It is a destination for global tourism and one of the city's biggest moneymakers. Commodities line the windows of almost every store and you'd be lucky to find a flat here that is under 4,000 dollars. A few years back, the residents of the Castro district refused to have a youth center be built in the neighborhood because it would "bring down property value," in their words. The Castro is the perfect symbol of the complete bankruptcy and co-optation of the Queer Rights movement. Tourism and profit stand over the lives and safety of youth who desperately need to escape from their abusive families. This is what happens when the Queers desire to become mainstream. It becomes an issue of "who can comfortably assimilate and who can't." And you can see what happens to those who can't.

My problem with the hype and pressure around DADT is that it distracts from the very things that the Queer Liberation movement was founded on: Anti-imperialism, anti-racism, equal access to housing and healthcare, and struggles against patriarchy. It seems almost irrelevant to me whether or not gay soldiers can "come out" in the military when the U.S. military is not only carrying out two genocidal campaigns for U.S. imperialism and corporate profit, but also when the war budget is draining the funds needed for almost every other service we so desperately need in this country. When I see the situation as such, not only does it become apparent to me that the Queer Movement must be anti-war, but also that the movement, as is, has been hijacked by a few high-powered assimilationists dragging everyone along through corporate propaganda.

So no, I will not be getting my tens in the Castro when DADT is struck down.

This piece was originally printed as a feature article in the October 2005 edition of The Guide, a gay travel magazine owned by Pink Triangle Press.

Pictures at an Execution
Bill Andriette

Sometimes photos pack such a punch that they're not just pictures of something, but also give off X-rays. Such photos yield secondary images — the shadows cast as the X-rays pass through the body-politic, revealing perhaps fractures, tumors, and clots otherwise unseen.

The bootleg snapshots from Abu Ghraib beamed such X-rays widely. The photos, you remember, depicted U.S. soldiers tormenting Iraqis held at Baghdad's infamous prison — piling them up naked, siccing dogs on them, mocking their corpses. But the corresponding X-ray image revealed as well a hidden abscess of brutality at U.S. prisons — day jobs at which a number of the reservist ring-leaders had just departed to fight in Iraq. In passing through the angry Muslim street, the X-rays revealed an intestinal blockage in Arab politics — for many Middle East rulers, sometimes not at the behest of American sponsors, had committed far more deadly atrocities against their people without thereby losing legitimacy. The X-rays as well showed a strange disconnect between the hemispheres in the Bush brain, which had ordered careful juridical defenses of torture on one hand, and yet expressed shock — shock! — that American soldiers might force conquered Iraqis to simulate cocksucking.

The photos taken July 19 of Iranian teenagers Mahmoud Asgari, 16, and Ayaz Marhoni, 18, about to be hanged for sodomy, also radiated X-rays. The images made only a brief appearance in the mainstream media. But for gay people, even a glance was liable to catch the eye, as if on a hook. The two youths were executed in Mashad, a city in northeast Iran, and had each been in custody 14 months. They confessed also to drinking, disturbing the peace, and theft. The youths had been tortured, at least by the 228 lashes they received before they were killed.

The photos produced various reactions — from calls to smash Iranian "Islamo-Fascism," to denunciations of executions of underage lawbreakers, to demands for an official U.S. investigation.

Yet the X-ray cast by the photos from Mashad also reveal contradictions in the Western gay body-politic and the human-rights groups that, by default, often serve as its foreign ministry.

What happened?

The fate of Mahmoud Asgari and Ayaz Marhoni is clear, but what led up to their hangings isn't. There are two versions — that their crimes consisted mainly of consensual sex, either together, or with another teenager, 13; or that the two assaulted the younger boy.

The photos accompanied a report in Farsi from the Iranian Student News Agency on July 19. OutRage!, a British gay group, noticed ISNA's dispatch on the web, and says it had the article translated by a native speaker. OutRage! says the ISNA account said the youths were executed for sodomy, claims repeated in English on two other Iranian web sites, one tied to an armed insurgent group fighting the Iranian state. On July 21, OutRage! issued a release: "Iran executes gay teenagers." Citing ISNA's interview with the youths as they were taken to the gallows, OutRage! noted that "They admitted (probably under torture) to having gay sex but claimed in their defense that most young boys had sex with each other and that they were not aware that homosexuality was punishable by death."

OutRage!'s report — and the shock of the photos — surged through the internet, and caught the notice of US gay groups that normally don't look much beyond American shores. Log Cabin Republicans and blogger Andrew Sullivan joined in expressing horror at the execution of the "gay teenagers." On Sullivan's blog, an unidentified soldier wrote that "Your post on the Islamo-fascist hanging/murder of the two gay men confirmed for me that my recent decision to join the U.S. military was correct. I have to stuff myself back in the closet... but our war on terror trumps my personal comfort at this point. Whenever my friends and family criticize — I'll show 'em that link." The Human Rights Campaign, along with some congressmen — Tom Lantos and openly-gay Barney Frank among them — called on the U.S. to investigate.

OutRage! contends that only subsequent news reports made other claims — that the two executed teenagers (when they were presumably aged 15 and 17) forced the other boy into sex. These allegations are not reliable, the group argues, but were likely concocted as a cover to blunt Western criticism. "It could be that the 13-year-old was a willing participant but that Iranian law (like the laws of many Western nations) deems that no person aged 13 is capable of sexual consent," says OutRage!'s Brett Lock, "and that therefore even consensual sexual contact is automatically deemed in law to be statutory rape."

Human Rights Watch (HRW) disputes key parts of OutRage!'s account. The original ISNA report uses an archaic term that suggests forced sodomy, says HRW's Scott Long, director of the group's GLBT rights project. And details about an assault appeared in a Mashad newspaper on the morning of the execution, before any Western protests. That report quotes the father of the alleged victim at length describing how his son was, he says, led from a shopping area in Mashad to a deserted alley where five other boys were waiting (they also face execution, but apparently have not been caught), and forced him to have sex at knife-point. Passersby, also quoted, say that when they tried to intervene, they and their cars were attacked.

By the time the pictures hit the mainstream Western media, the story was about executions for rape — and official interest dampened. The Human Rights Campaign briefly removed mention of the case from its website, and spokesman Steven Fisher told *The Nation*, "We would be relieved to learn that the charges of homosexual sex were wrong, and that this turned out to be a case of assault." The U.S. State Department issued a statement criticizing the Iranian judiciary for its mingling of prosecutorial and judicial functions, among other alleged shortcomings, mentioning nothing about its oppression of homosexuals.

Mainline human-rights groups, including Amnesty International and the International Gay and Lesbian Human Rights Commission (IGLHRC), agreed with the U.S. line that the Mashad executions were not gay-related. But they should be condemned, these groups said, on the grounds that the youths were minors when put to death or when they committed the crimes for which they were convicted.

Paula Ettelbrick, IGLHRC's director, cites a litany of cases — including Iran's execution of a 16-year-old girl, Atefeh Rajabi, last August for "acts incompatible with chastity" — as showing that Iran is capable of hanging and stoning people simply for consensual sex, so recourse to made-up tales of coercion wasn't necessary.

However, Ettelbrick also expressed concern at what she felt was "language having the potential to be racially/religiously charged" that OutRage! spokespeople and others were using to characterize Iran.

"Skepticism about official accounts in any country with a record of rights violations — be it Iran or the U.S. — is merited," writes HRW's Long, "and no one under these circumstances would claim total certainty that consensual sex was not involved. But the basis for believing that the boys were convicted of consensual sex is essentially a web of speculation."

"Rights aren't for saints, and if we only defend them for people onto whom we can project our own qualities, our own identities, we aren't activists but narcissists with attitude," Long goes on. "If these kids aren't 'gay,' or 'innocent,' but are 'straight' or 'guilty,' does it make their fear less horrible, their suffering less real? Does it make them less dead?"

OutRage! still insists the hangings were, whatever else, also anti-gay, and emanations of what it regards as a hateful regime. Threat of severe punishment hung over all the boys involved — including the one characterized as the victim. Reports from witnesses and the teenager's father about assault at knife-point could stem as much as anything from a desire to save his son's life or reputation. Sex among young Iranian males is, on many accounts, commonplace — sometimes through trickery or bullying that falls along a spectrum from the gameful to the cruel. Authorities might have concocted an account of coercion not because they needed it to prosecute or execute, but because otherwise, the scenario of boys having sex together would have seemed too ordinary. The statement by the doomed youths on the way to their execution that they didn't know what they did could lead to execution makes less sense if they were involved in a gang rape at knife-point, and more plausible if it was mere homosex, or some kind of sex-tinged hazing.

In addition, the executed youths were ethnic Arabs from Khuzestan, one of Iran's ethnic minorities in longstanding conflict with Iran's Persian Shiite majority. Khuzestan abuts the Iraqi border, and many Arabs had been forced to migrate during the Iran-Iraq war, the families of the executed teenagers among them. Iranian authorities-- as elsewhere — have smeared members of ethnic minorities whom they've targeted with sexual innuendo. In a report on the killing by security forces July 9 of a Kurdish activist, Shivan Qaderi, HRW's website notes that authorities accused him of "moral and financial violations."

Certainly in another recent case, the commingling of sodomy and rape charges has the ring of implausibility. In Arak, 150 miles south of Tehran, at the end of August,

two men — Farad Mostar and Ahmed Choka, both 27 —
were reportedly set to be executed for what was alleged as
the sequestering and rape of another man, 22.

Back in Mashad, Asgari and Marhoni may indeed have
coerced another teenager into sex — HRW says they are
"90 percent" sure. But there were also plenty of hooks by
which highly interested parties might have transformed a
fairly innocent act into a seemingly more monstrous one.

If Western media interest in the youths' case faltered once
it was characterized as assault, the images of the hangings
could not be erased from the gay imagination. The Dutch
gay group COC collected almost 30,000 signatures on an
on-line petition, and protests were held, among other
places, in London, Moscow, Paris, and Vancouver.

America = Iran?

So in the aftermath of the hangings, everything went
about as well as could be expected, right? Newspapers
reported, bloggers blogged, protests broke out, and
politicians queried. Militant gay activists ventured further
out on their thicker limbs with bold speculation, while
human-rights groups stuck cautiously, as they should, to
the main trunk of proof and principle. Even the potshots
each sometimes took at the other were just signs of
healthy debate.

Yet a closer look shows abounding contradictions and
blind-spots. Everyone who responded arguably got key
points seriously wrong, so that the cumulative effect
wasn't to erase the errors but amplify them.

Asgari and Marhoni were terribly unlucky to have done
what they did in Iran, but even on the most benign

reading of their actions, they would have fared only a little better in America. Under the toxic bloom of anti-sex laws in the last generation — but especially the last decade, intimately connected to the mainstreaming of vanilla LGBT — the youths would have faced years in prison, and in some ways effectively guaranteed life sentences. They would have fallen into a separate-and-unequal legal netherworld that has developed around sex law that bears comparison to that created to control African-Americans in the post-Civil-War South.

Authorities have not yet figured out a way to dye sex-offenders' skin permanently scarlet — but Asgari and Marhoni, as residents of Memphis instead of Mashad — would have been labeled as "predators" for the rest of their lives — and depending on the precise jurisdiction (though all are now racing to the bottom) their pictures and addresses of home and workplace (assuming they had either) would be forever posted on the internet, shown regularly on TV, and plastered on posters around their neighborhoods. The electronic tags they'd be forced to wear — or on scenarios now being worked out, the chips that would be implanted in their bodies — would track their location constantly — so that police could always find them. Or outraged citizens — as happened August 27, when a man posing as an FBI agent came to the home where three registered sex-offenders lived in Bellingham, Washington, and shot two of them dead, one of them a gay man, 49-year-old Hank Eisses, convicted in 1997 of sex with a teenage boy. Eisses did not exactly become the next Matthew Shepard: the murders were barely noticed by the media.

But more and more, the impulse is to keep people convicted of illegal sex in the West forever in prison. In 1997, five years before Guantanamo Bay, the U.S.

Supreme Court established that persons, convicted or not, can be imprisoned indefinitely for illegal sex they might have in the future — a provision that was only later applied to those labeled terrorists. If sex-offenders do get out of prison, they take the ball and chain with them. Lifetime parole — which gradually most U.S. states are adopting, as a natural extension of the registries — gives probation officers a level of complete personal control over their charges not seen since serfdom. Authorities can send their charges back to prison for failing a lie-detector test, possessing a copy of *The Best Gay Short Stories of 1995* (a case in York City), having too much candy in the cupboard (one in California), or passing too close to a school (Baltimore, Maryland).

You don't have to be a sociopathic rapist to feel the brunt of the repression. Gay men whose erotic profile bears resemblance to Oscar Wilde, Walt Whitman, André Gide, or Alan Turing are in danger. Anyone who has a 1960's physique magazine with teenage models in posing straps, or who gropes a bearded 17-year-old who's cruising at a rest-stop is at risk. Indeed, the range of people affected is even bigger, because sex-offenders in the West have become guinea pigs for technologies of biometric and electronic surveillance-and-tracking that increasingly, under the guise of fighting terror, are rolled out for everyone.

A child leads them?

Rather than confronting these realities — which in any case they've completely ignored — human rights groups responding to the Iranian hangings, in a sense, gave in to them. Killing Asgari and Marhoni was wrong, Human Rights Watch and IGLHRC said, because they were executions of "children," or, in Marhon's case, someone who offended when he was a "child." In other words, the executions were wrong for the same reason the two criminals were, in the eyes of most Westerners today, deserving of utmost punishment. Thus was indulged one of the West's great current conceits — the child as the central category of moral discourse and a primary justification of repression. The concept of the "child" absurdly lumps two-year-olds, eight-year-olds, and seventeen-year-olds — and increasingly twenty-somethings — into the same essential category of sub-person. This is a conceit to which Iran — which grants the vote to 15-year-olds even as it allows their execution — is far less in thrall.

Human-rights groups understandably played the child-card in service to their principled opposition to the death penalty. Iran is a party to the Convention on the Rights of the Child, which commits it not to execute juvenile offenders, so this was a chance to make an argument that might have practical effect. But even here, the approach was something of a cop-out. While the execution of young lawbreakers may be a wedge into the main point — against states executing anybody — it is also a distraction from it. In the same way, a campaign to spare the lives of puppies at the dog-pound may serve as entree to increasing people's concern about the web of bacteria, insects, plants, and animals that sustains an ecosystem. Or it may just impart the lesson that only adorable life-forms have reason to exist.

Doing good, doing well

Which raises the question of how much human-rights groups focus on "what's sexy" rather than what's principled. In their principles, in their equal regard for all persons, the human rights movement enjoys enormous global prestige — akin the status of Catholicism in medieval Europe, or socialism before the taint of Stalin and Mao. Human rights is the successor to the best of what, in their heyday, these universalist projects stood for. In the post-'60s West, perhaps the only more-successful movements are those centered around various identities — such as race, sex, and sexuality. The two tendencies are different — sometimes diametrically — and each is tempted to draw on the unique strengths of the other. Hence, perhaps, Human Rights Watch's elevation, as shown on its website, of same-sex marriage to a basic human-right — while ignoring, say, any right to polygamy, or other matrimonial arrangements to which people might freely contract.

Certainly mainline gay groups fail to protest civil-commitment laws, kiddie-porn statutes the likes of Canada's just-passed Bill C-2 — a law that, in removing the "artistic merit" provision, makes possessing a book of, say, 16th-century Persian Safavid boy-love poems punishable by up to 10 years in prison. Human Rights Watch, in a nod to the identity movements whose success it must envy, joins in the silence.

To be sure, groups such as Amnesty International and Human Rights Watch do vital work, and mostly hew to their principles, avoiding the short-termist excitability that goes with the territory of identity-politics. The prestige of these groups is largely deserved. However, it's just this prestige the U.S. aims to cash in on when it claims that its smart bombs and bunker-busters are the greatest force ever assembled for promotion of, as is continually intoned, "democracy and human rights." But as well, the human-rights cause risks death-by-a-thousand-cuts when special interests wrap themselves in its mantle.

A classic instance is America's Human Rights Campaign, which puts the magic phrase into its name (even if only to avoid saying "gay"), but "doesn't have a position" on what is one of human rights most basic planks — against execution. Being a pure-play lesbigay organization has helped make HRC the biggest and richest in America. The really fat donors don't want tearoom cruisers and drag queens (let alone the class of folk stuck last month in the Superdome) spoiling their high-Episcopal gay weddings.

Ettelbrick expresses surprise that HRC would issue public statements about the Iranian hangings without consulting the human-rights groups that have some depth in that part of the world. But that misses the successful political arbitrage HRC pulled off — selling the photo from Mashad long when it had huge political value as depicting "Brutal Islamic Execution of Gay Teens" and buying it short when the caption was "Pedo Rapists Get Just Desserts."

It was the same trick played by Rep. Tom Lantos, who demanded a U.S. investigation into the hangings and lambasted Iran's treatment of gays, but voted for the 2003 PROTECT Act, under which an American Asgari or Marhoni could face years in federal prison — not for raping a teenager, not for having consensual sex with him, but merely calling him on a cell phone (think "interstate commerce") with the intention of arranging to "hook up." (Barney Frank, to his credit, voted nay.)

But if identity politics often conflicts with the demands of human rights, it was the militant identistas of UK's OutRage! who demonstrated the best grasp of the human dynamics of the case. Yet OutRage!'s portrayal of Asgari and Marhoni as "gay teenagers" is off-the-mark. They evidently, like many young Iranian males, enjoyed same-sex activity, but "Did the hanged kids claim 'gay' identity?" asks journalist Doug Ireland. "Most probably not — since the concept is virtually unknown among the uneducated classes in Iran."

Yet Ireland is wrong, as well, to make gayness an ID every same-sexer would embrace if only he had cash and a diploma. Most Islamic societies allow ample space for unspoken and private homoeroticism. Amnesty International and IGLHRC have waged campaigns protesting crackdowns on gay Egyptian hookup sites — which serve only the tiny and westernized elite who have net access. But one effect is to increase scrutiny on the unmarked homosexual spaces on which most Egyptians with same-sex desires depend.

Which leads Joseph Massad, historian at Columbia and author of the forthcoming *Desiring Arabs*, to wonder whether gay and human-rights groups really care about same-sex love and affection, in its diverse forms, around the world. Because with such campaigns, Massad declares, "the 'Gay International' is destroying social and sexual configurations of desire in the interest of reproducing a world in its own image, one wherein its sexual categories and desires are safe from being questioned."

Reforming Islam

If protesting anti-gay crackdowns from afar has perverse effects for Islamic homosociality, all the more so when Westerners actually invade. Which makes the pride Andrew Sullivan's gay soldier feels bitterly ironic. In post-Saddam Iraq, power lies with the majority Shiites, who have forged warm ties to Tehran. Iran's victory in Iraq was delivered by its arch-enemies America and Iraq's

Sunni Arabs — the first by deposing the secularist Saddam, the second in resisting the Americans, bogging them down, and preventing Stage Two of the neo-con agenda: a march to Tehran.

But step back further and the irony of Western intervention is even more bitter and hugely sadder. Time after time, Islamic modernizers were deposed by Western powers, starting with the British in India, and continuing in Iran with the CIA's overthrow of the democratically-elected Mohammad Mosaddeq in 1953, with the subsequent imposition of the Shah Pahlevi. Islamic fundamentalism may seem today immensely potent, but — from Afghanistan to Gaza — it's usually been a politics of last resort.

In Iran, gayness can't avoid some odor of colonial occupation. "Not all the accusations leveled against the Pahlevi family and their wealthy supporters stemmed from political and economic grievances," notes Ireland, citing Iranian scholar Janet Afary. "A significant portion of the public anger was aimed at their 'immoral' lifestyle. There were rumors that a gay lifestyle was rampant at the court. The Shah himself was rumored to be bisexual. There were reports that a close male friend of the Shah from Switzerland, a man who knew him from their student days in that country, routinely visited him."

Post-revolutionary Iran, for all its bloody repression, had also shown signs of thaw — there was a reformist president and an emerging gay-activist underground. "The GLBT situation in Iran has changed over the past 26 years," says an unnamed activist interviewed on www.gayrussia.ru/en after the executions. "The regime does not systematically persecute gays anymore. There are still some gay websites, there are some parks and cinemas that everyone knows are meeting places for gays. Furthermore, it is legal in Iran that a transsexual applies for sex-change, and it is fully accepted by the government. Having said that, Islamic law, according to which gays face punishment by death, is still in force, but it is thought not much followed by the regime nowadays."

That may be changing, with a right-wing resurgence, egged on by U.S. threats, and exemplified by the election this summer of Mahmoud Ahmadinejad — whose authoritarian puritanism may be linked to the uptick in sodomy executions.

And Iran's nuclear ambitions, the rationale for the U.S. saber-rattling, are relevant as well. Iran chose its nuclear course, argues Joost Hilterman, after what happened in its eight-year-long war with then-U.S.-sponsored Iraq, when Iranian troops were bombarded with Saddam's chemical weapons. When Iran protested and invoked international agreements on their illegality, the U.S. balked, and cooked up phony evidence showing Iran — not client-state Iraq — as the chemical-weapons perp. "The young and inexperienced Islamic Republic learned from its experience [that] when you are facing the world's superpower, multilateral treaties and conventions are worthless," notes Hilterman in *Middle East Report*. Only military self-sufficiency could guard its independence. And indeed, all that Iran has aimed at so far — mastery of the nuclear fuel-cycle — is within its rights under the UN's anti-proliferation treaty. But still the country faces a U.S. attack — possibly a nuclear one — under rules that America has unilaterally changed mid-course.

So Iranians are alive to imperial self-interest and bigotry masked in the flowery language of universal principle.

They also know that on sexual perversion — in the different ways each defines it — America and Iran see eye-to-eye.

Seeing the photograph of Mahmoud Asgari and Ayaz Marhoni in tears before they died on the scaffold gives many of us a terrible urge to do something. Yet that image yields another — cast by the X-rays it shines upon the organs and metabolic pathways of the Western body-politic. The X-ray offers an inner-view of the organizations, principles, and conceptual categories that we have at-hand to act on that urge to "do something." And that's where we find ourselves at a further loss, facing an organism that is artery-clogged, cataract-ridden, and palsied. Like a doddering old man trying to drink tea but spilling it everywhere, the gap between cup and lip seems for now insurmountable.

These following cartoons have appeared in numerous places online and in print. They are archived on Truthdig.com and Mr. Fish's own website, clowncrack.com.

Illustrating Against Militarism
Mr. Fish

Three of Mr. Fish's sassy and incisive cartoons focused on militarism and sexuality appear on the following pages. We've spread them out so that you can easily rip out the pages with images, enlarge them on a photocopier or scanner, and disseminate in your own community without losing any pages of text!

DON'T ASK ME TO SUBMIT TO VIGOROUS TRAINING THAT SUBVERTS
MY NATURAL INCLINATIONS TOWARDS COMPASSION, HOPE, OPTIM-
ISM AND COMMON SENSE SO THAT I AM ENTHUSIASTIC ABOUT
TERRORIZING OTHER NATIONS BY INVADING AND OCCUPYING THEM
DAY IN AND DAY OUT, YEAR AFTER YEAR AFTER YEAR, AND THEN BY
ABDUCTING AND TORTURING THEIR INNOCENT DAY IN AND DAY OUT,
YEAR AFTER YEAR AFTER YEAR, AND THEN BY SLAUGHTERING MAS-
SIVE AMOUNTS OF THEIR DEFENSELESS CIVILIANS DAY IN AND DAY
OUT, YEAR AFTER YEAR AFTER YEAR, AND I WON'T GIVE A SHIT
ABOUT HOW THE IDEA OF TWO MEN HUGGING AND KISSING MIGHT
TURN YOUR STOMACH.

MR FISH

77

About the Contributors

Bill Andriette has written for and edited a number of gay periodicals and for 20 years was an editor at *The Guide*, a Boston-based gay magazine shut down by its new owners, Toronto's Pink Triangle Press, in 2010. His work has appeared in such places as *Gay Community News*, *Playboy*, and *Newsday*, and he founded and edited *Gayme*. He studied philosophy at Cornell University, and has written on the intersection of sexuality and economics and the role of sexual demonization as a leitmotif of contemporary Western state legitimacy. He has come to take a dim view of 'LGBT' identity politics as a function of Western neoliberal, neo-imperialist, neo-totalitarian tendencies.

Ryan Conrad is an outlaw artist, terrorist academic, and petty thief from a mill town in central Maine. He works through visual culture and performance to rupture the queer here and now in hopes of making time and space to imagine the most fantastic queer futures. His visual work is archived at www.faggotz.org and he is a member of the editorial collective for *Against Equality*. He can be reached at rconrad@meca.edu.

Kenyon Farrow is the former Executive Director of Queers for Economic Justice, an organization that does community organizing, leadership development, research and advocacy with, and on issues that impact, low-income and working class LGBTQ people. As a writer, Kenyon is a regular contributor to TheGrio.com. He is also the co-editor of Letters from *Young Activists: Today's Rebels Speak Out* (Nation Books), and the forthcoming *Stand Up!: The Politics of Racial Uplift* (South End Press).

Larry Goldsmith is a historian and a former reporter for *Gay Community News* (Boston, Massachusetts), and has been active in anti-war, labor, and LGBT organizations since the late 1970s. He lives in Mexico City, and teaches at the Universidad Nacional Autónoma de México and El Colegio de México.

Jamal Rashad Jones is a Oakland transplant, originally from Washington, DC. Growing up poor, Black and Queer in D.C. meant dealing with the issues of racism, and state violence in addition to patriarchy. Struggling with all of these factors brought together his current politics. In 2011, he graduated from SF State with a BA in Africana studies and a passion for politics, art, and revolution. Currently he teaches creative writing and visual arts in East Oakland and spends his spare time developing different autonomous, Marxist, queer spaces, and the art collective that he is a member of, The Corner Collective. In the future, he would like to continue to express himself through writing and help to be a part of the movement for a new society. He believes that class antagonisms are high and the time is now to organize the world we wish to see.

82

Cecilia Cissell Lucas lives in Oakland and is a student/teacher at UC Berkeley, working on a dissertation about reparations as an approach to racial justice. She received her BFA in Theater and subsequently spent almost five years working as the Assistant Director of Albany Park Theater Project, creating plays with an ensemble of youth and adult artists based on real-life stories of Chicago's Albany Park neighborhood. These days she stays connected to the arts world by playing taiko, dancing, and going to as many performances as her student loans will allow. She also occasionally writes analyses of current events (published by *CommonDreams*, *MRZine*, *CounterPunch*, *Dissident Voice*, and Against Equality), has been a bus manager for Wheels of Justice, and played/plays a supportive role in various social justice projects.

Erica R. Meiners writes about her collaborative learning and work in *Social Justice, Meridians, Monthly Review, Radical Teacher, AREA Chicago,* and *Women's Studies Quarterly.* Into long distance running, looking after her bees, prison abolition and reading science fiction, she is a 2011-2012 Visiting Research Professor at the Institute for Research on Race and Public Policy at the University of Illinois at Chicago. She is also a Professor of Education, Women's Studies and Latino and Latin American Studies at Northeastern Illinois University in Chicago, where she is a member of her labor union, University Professionals of Illinois (UPI Local 4100).

Mr. Fish has been a freelance writer and cartoonist for eighteen years, publishing under both his real name (Dwayne Booth) and the pen name of Mr. Fish with many of the nation's most reputable and prestigious magazines, journals, and newspapers. In addition to his weekly cartoon for *Harper's* and daily contributions to

Truthdig.com, he has also contributed to the *Los Angeles Times*, the *Village Voice*, the *LA Weekly*, the *Atlantic*, the *Nation*, the *Huffington Post*, *Vanity Fair, Mother Jones*, the *Advocate, Z Magazine*, the *Utne Reader*, Slate.com, MSNBC.com, and others. He has also worked for National Public Radio. In May 2008 he was presented with a first place award by the Los Angeles Press Club for editorial cartooning. In both 2010 and 2011 he was awarded the prestigious Sigma Delta Chi Award for Editorial Cartooning from the Society of Professional Journalists. He lives in Philadelphia with his wife and twin daughters.

Yasmin Nair is a Chicago-based writer, activist, academic, and commentator and a co-founder of Against Equality. The bastard child of queer theory and deconstruction, Nair's work has appeared in publications like *GLQ, The Progressive, make/shift, Time Out Chicago*, The Bilerico Project, *Windy City Times, Bitch, Maximum Rock'n'Roll*, and *No More Potlucks*. Her work also appears in various anthologies and journals, including *Captive Genders: Trans Embodiment and the Prison Industrial Complex, Singlism: What It Is, Why It Matters and How to Stop It, Windy City Queer: Dispatches from the Third Coast and Arab Studies Quarterly*. She is also a member of the Chicago grassroots organization Gender JUST (Justice United for Societal Transformation). Nair is currently working on a book tentatively titled *Strange Love*, about neoliberalism and affect. Her website is www.yasminnair.net.

Tamara K. Nopper is an Asian American woman with a PhD in sociology. She has activist experience in immigrant rights and counter-military recruitment work. She teaches courses on and writes about race and ethnic relations, immigration, labor and entrepreneurship, and Asian American communities.

Therese Quinn is Chair and Associate Professor of Art Education at the School of the Art Institute of Chicago. Her most recent books, all collaborative projects, are *Teaching Toward Democracy* (Paradigm, 2010), *Flaunt It! Queers Organizing for Public Education and Justice* (Peter Lang, 2009), and *Handbook of Social Justice in Education* (Routledge, 2009). She co-edits the Teachers College Press Series, *Teaching for Social Justice*, writes a column for *Yliopisto*, the magazine of the University of Helsinki, and grows gooseberries, raspberries and roses.

Mattilda Bernstein Sycamore is most recently the editor of *Why Are Faggots So Afraid of Faggots?: Flaming Challenges to Masculinity, Objectification, and the Desire to Conform*, out on Valentine's Day 2012 from AK Press — the perfect romantic gift! Mattilda is the author of two novels, most recently *So Many Ways to Sleep Badly* (City Lights 2008), and the editor of four additional nonfiction anthologies, including *Nobody Passes: Rejecting the Rules of Gender and Conformity* (Seal 2007) and an expanded second edition of *That's Revolting! Queer Strategies for Resisting Assimilation* (Soft Skull 2008). Mattilda's first memoir, *The End of San Francisco*, will devastate the world soon. Mattilda loves feedback and propositions, so always feel free to contact her via mattildabernsteinsycamore.com.